United States Government Accountability Office

Report to Congressional Requesters

I0448814

September 2013

DHS RECRUITING AND HIRING

DHS Is Generally Filling Mission-Critical Positions, but Could Better Track Costs of Coordinated Recruiting Efforts

GAO Highlights

Highlights of GAO-13-742, a report to congressional requesters

DHS RECRUITING AND HIRING

DHS Is Generally Filling Mission-Critical Positions, but Could Better Track Costs of Coordinated Recruiting Efforts

Why GAO Did This Study

With more than 240,000 employees doing diverse jobs, DHS's workforce supports the department's multiple missions to prevent terrorism and enhance security and ensure resilience from disasters, amongst others. Given these missions, it is important that DHS effectively recruit and hire employees with the appropriate skills. Within DHS, the Office of the Chief Human Capital Officer (OCHCO) is responsible for human capital policy development and implementation. GAO has previously reported on DHS's challenges in attracting and retaining a qualified workforce. GAO was asked to assess DHS's recruiting and hiring strategies. This report addresses the extent to which (1) DHS and four selected components have implemented recruiting and hiring strategies to fill MCOs, and (2) DHS has assessed these efforts. To conduct its work, GAO reviewed recruiting strategies and data on MCO hiring and losses, and interviewed officials from OCHCO and the four DHS components selected for this review based on their varieties of MCOs and recruiting strategies. Information from these components cannot be generalized to all of DHS, but provides insights.

What GAO Recommends

GAO recommends that DHS require all components to provide recruiting cost information in a consistent manner. DHS concurred with GAO's recommendation.

View GAO-13-742. For more information, contact David C. Maurer at (202) 512-9627 or maurerd@gao.gov.

What GAO Found

The Department of Homeland Security (DHS) and selected components are implementing strategies to fill mission-critical occupations (MCO), which are those occupations most critical to an agency's mission. In 2011, the Office of Diversity and Inclusion (D&I)—which coordinates component recruiting efforts—developed the *Coordinated Recruiting and Outreach Strategy* (CROS). Through the CROS, D&I intends to better coordinate and link component recruiting and outreach efforts to hiring for DHS mission and workforce needs (for all positions, including MCOs), and to leverage resources as well as reduce recruiting costs, among other things. D&I has begun to implement the CROS through various means, including requiring components to develop their own outreach and recruiting plans that align with the CROS. However, D&I has been limited in its ability to implement some elements of the CROS—such as recruiter training—because of budget constraints, according to D&I officials. The components selected for GAO's review—the National Protection and Programs Directorate, Transportation Security Administration (TSA), U.S. Citizenship and Immigration Services, and U.S. Secret Service (USSS)—have also implemented various strategies to recruit and hire MCOs. In addition, these four components have generally been able to address hiring needs for MCOs. For example, USSS data show that vacancy rates were generally below 3 percent for MCO positions during fiscal years 2010 through 2012. Still, some officials have reported experiencing challenges attracting qualified candidates because of factors such as financial constraints and regional competition, among other things. For example, TSA has been challenged in filling certain positions in some areas where competition for other jobs makes it difficult to attract qualified candidates.

D&I is taking steps to assess implementation of the CROS, but could improve efforts to track recruiting costs. D&I assesses progress in implementing the CROS by tracking and monitoring component performance for six measures, such as compliance with data-tracking requirements. These measures are aligned with the two overarching goals of the CROS; however, they do not include targets to measure DHS's progress in achieving the goals over the period the strategy covers (2012–2017). D&I officials stated that they are gathering baseline data on these measures and plan to use these data to help develop targets in the future. In addition, three of the CROS's six annual measures are associated with its goal of recruiting a highly qualified workforce. However, DHS does not require components to report the information needed to accurately assess component performance for one of these measures—which calls for standardized data tracking of recruiting and outreach activities. D&I has developed a database for components to use to track recruiting efforts and costs, but it does not require that all components use this tool or provide data to DHS in a consistent manner. D&I officials said that since some components have their own tracking systems, they do not want the tracking systems to duplicate efforts. D&I acknowledges the importance of obtaining comprehensive and consistent cost information from components, but has not determined whether and how it will do so. As a result, D&I does not know the total amount of money being spent on recruiting and outreach throughout DHS, nor is it able to fully track component recruiting costs—and therefore cannot measure the results of the second goal in the CROS of optimizing outreach and recruiting resources.

_____ United States Government Accountability Office

Contents

Figure

Abbreviations

CRC	Corporate Recruiting Council
CROS	*Coordinated Recruiting and Outreach Strategy*
CS&C	Office of Cybersecurity and Communications
CSORP	Component Specific Outreach and Recruiting Plan
D&I	Office of Diversity and Inclusion
DHS	Department of Homeland Security
FPS	Federal Protective Service
GPRA	Government Performance and Results Act
ISO	immigration services officer
IT	information technology
LEO	law enforcement officer
MCO	mission-critical occupation
NPPD	National Protection and Programs Directorate
OCHCO	Office of the Chief Human Capital Officer
OPM	Office of Personnel Management
TSA	Transportation Security Administration
TSO	transportation security officer
USCIS	U.S. Citizenship and Immigration Services
USSS	U.S. Secret Service

GAO U.S. GOVERNMENT ACCOUNTABILITY OFFICE

441 G St. N.W.
Washington, DC 20548

September 17, 2013

Congressional Requesters

The Department of Homeland Security (DHS) is the third-largest cabinet-level department in the federal government, with over 240,000 employees doing diverse jobs covering aviation and border security, emergency response, cybersecurity analysis, and chemical facility inspection.[1] To address the increasingly complex national security challenges associated with its wide array of responsibilities, it is important that DHS have programs and policies in place to effectively recruit and hire employees with the appropriate skills to meet its various mission requirements. In recent years, we, the Office of Personnel Management (OPM), and other parties have identified major challenges to recruitment and hiring in the federal government broadly and at DHS specifically, such as passive recruitment strategies and insufficient workforce planning. For example, passive recruitment strategies, such as infrequent or no outreach to college campuses, can create missed opportunities to expose potential employees to information about federal jobs. Also, we have found that federal agencies made limited use of hiring flexibilities that could better position them to efficiently hire well-qualified candidates for jobs.[2] We have also reported that in order to ensure that organizations are reaching out to diverse pools of talent, agencies must consider active recruitment strategies, such as widening the selection of schools from which they recruit, building formal relationships with targeted schools and colleges to ensure the cultivation of talent for future applicant pools, and partnering with multicultural professional organizations and speaking at their conferences to communicate their commitment to diversity to external audiences and strengthen and maintain relationships.

Specific to DHS, we have reported that the department faces challenges in attracting and retaining a qualified workforce, particularly in the areas of acquisitions, information technology, and cybersecurity. For example, in

---

[1]This total includes military staff in the U.S. Coast Guard and intelligence-related positions. Our review generally focuses on civilian, nonintelligence personnel, which results in a total of approximately 200,000 DHS employees.

[2]GAO, *Human Capital: Transforming Federal Recruiting and Hiring Efforts*, GAO-08-762T (Washington, D.C.: May 8, 2008). This report addresses recruiting and hiring efforts across the federal government, and includes work reviewing DHS.

November 2011, we reported on workforce planning challenges for cybersecurity personnel in the federal government.[3] We found, among other things, that the agencies we analyzed—including DHS—faced challenges in filling these highly technical occupations. In addition, our work in identifying high-risk areas in the federal government has identified DHS management, including the function of human capital management, as a high-risk area. In a September 2010 letter to DHS based on our prior work, we reported on the need for DHS to develop and demonstrate sustained progress in implementing a recruiting and hiring strategy that is targeted to fill both short- and long-term needs, and specifically to fill identified human capital gaps, including diversity and foreign language gaps.

Under the authority of DHS's Office of the Chief Human Capital Officer (OCHCO), DHS's Office of Diversity and Inclusion (D&I) provides department-wide leadership and guidance on diversity and inclusion management related to recruitment and outreach, career development, and workforce inclusion, among other things.[4] DHS's components operate within the human capital framework established and overseen by OCHCO, and their respective component-level human capital offices, or their equivalents, work with DHS OCHCO to manage human capital efforts at each of the components.

The process of recruiting and hiring involves developing and implementing strategies to advertise positions and attract top candidates as well as assessing applicants' relative competencies or knowledge, skills, and abilities against job-related criteria to identify the most qualified candidates to potentially hire. This includes identifying mission-critical occupations (MCO), which are those occupations that most directly affect an agency's ability to perform its mission, and determining the specific skills and competencies required to meet both current and future programmatic needs. At DHS, MCOs constitute a large proportion of the workforce, highlighting the importance of an effective DHS recruiting and hiring strategy to ensure these critical occupations are filled.

---

[3]GAO, *Cybersecurity Human Capital: Initiatives Need Better Planning and Coordination*, GAO-12-8 (Washington, D.C.: Nov. 29, 2011).

[4]In addition, D&I manages departmental efforts to increase the employment of veterans within DHS, and also leads efforts to investigate allegations of workplace harassment and provide resolution and corrective action when appropriate and necessary.

Given the importance of recruiting and hiring to DHS's mission to prevent terrorism, secure our borders and cyberspace, and ensure resilience to disasters, you asked us to assess DHS's recruiting and hiring strategies. This report addresses (1) the extent to which DHS and selected components have implemented recruiting and hiring strategies to fill MCOs, and (2) the extent to which DHS has assessed these efforts.

To address the extent to which DHS and selected components have implemented recruiting and hiring strategies to fill MCOs, we reviewed DHS's primary recruiting strategy—the *Coordinated Recruiting and Outreach Strategy* (CROS) for fiscal years 2012-2017—and OCHCO's efforts to facilitate implementation of the CROS among DHS's components. To gain an understanding of component efforts to address CROS provisions, as well as component efforts to develop and implement their own recruiting and hiring strategies, we selected four DHS components—the National Protection and Programs Directorate (NPPD), the Transportation Security Administration (TSA), the U.S. Citizenship and Immigration Services (USCIS), and the U.S. Secret Service (USSS)—and reviewed documentation developed in response to the CROS as well as their respective recruiting and hiring strategies.[5] We selected these components because they provided a cross section of varied missions, critical occupations, and recruiting strategies within DHS. For example, NPPD contains many of DHS's cybersecurity personnel—who hold positions for which DHS has faced challenges in recruiting and hiring in recent years. Though the results of our review of these components cannot be generalized to DHS as a whole, they provide valuable insights into recruiting and hiring efforts and challenges within

---

[5]DHS has seven operational components—Customs and Border Protection, Federal Emergency Management Agency, Immigration and Customs Enforcement, TSA, U.S. Coast Guard, USCIS, USSS—as well as NPPD, the Federal Law Enforcement Training Center, and several headquarters offices, for which OCHCO largely provides personnel processing. Within NPPD, there are four different subcomponents: Federal Protective Service (FPS), Office of Cybersecurity and Communications (CS&C), Office of Infrastructure Protection, and Office of Biometric Identity Management (which has replaced the United States Visitor and Immigration Status Indicator Technology program as of March 2013). FPS is a federal law enforcement agency that provides integrated security and law enforcement services to federally owned and leased buildings, facilities, properties, and other assets. CS&C is responsible for enhancing the security, resilience, and reliability of the nation's cyber and communications infrastructure. The Office of Biometric Identity Management provides biometric identification services that help federal, state, and local government decision makers accurately identify the people they encounter and determine whether those people pose a risk to the United States.

the department. In addition to reviewing these components' efforts to adhere to the CROS and develop their own recruiting strategies, we also analyzed workforce hiring data when available and appropriate.[6] To determine the reliability of these data, we reviewed documentation on the data systems and interviewed officials responsible for working with the data systems. Through this work, we determined these data were sufficiently reliable for our purposes. To gain further insights into the development of recruiting strategies and efforts, challenges faced in hiring for MCOs, and efforts to mitigate such challenges, we interviewed OCHCO officials responsible for overseeing department-wide recruiting and hiring strategies and efforts, and human capital officials in the four components included in our review at their headquarters and at selected field locations. We selected the four field locations based on input from the DHS components, who identified the regional offices that experienced successes or challenges in recruiting and hiring.[7] While the views and information shared by these components' regional representatives cannot be generalized to all regions or employees within each component, they provide insight into field-level recruiting and hiring experiences.

To address the extent to which DHS has assessed efforts to implement the CROS, we assessed DHS's efforts to ensure that components complied with reporting provisions of the CROS by reviewing documentation (such as component-specific strategies) prepared in response to the CROS, and also compared elements of the CROS with leading practices for workforce planning identified in our prior work, as

---

[6]As discussed later in this report, components use a variety of data to monitor and assess the success of their recruiting and hiring efforts. To provide illustrative examples of these data, we present the following information in this report: TSA hires and losses from fiscal years 2010 through 2012; USSS hires, losses, and vacancy rates from fiscal years 2010 through March of 2013; USCIS hires and losses through April of fiscal year 2013, as well as the number of qualified applications received during 2012; and NPPD hires and losses from fiscal years 2010 through May of 2013, as well as vacancy rates for the CS&C subcomponent and number of FPS officers as of June 2013.

[7]Specifically, we spoke with USCIS officials in Texas, USSS officials in New York, and TSA officials at airports in Colorado and Alaska.

well as general strategic planning.[8] We supplemented this review by interviewing OCHCO officials responsible for ensuring implementation of the CROS, as well as component officials who have worked with OCHCO in implementing this strategy.

We conducted this performance audit from November 2012 to September 2013 in accordance with generally accepted government auditing standards. Those standards require that we plan and perform the audit to obtain sufficient, appropriate evidence to provide a reasonable basis for our findings and conclusions based on our audit objectives. We believe that the evidence obtained provides a reasonable basis for our findings and conclusions based on our audit objectives.

Background

Federal Recruiting and Hiring Process

Recruiting and hiring involves developing and implementing strategies to advertise positions and attract top candidates as well as assessing applicants' relative competencies or knowledge, skills, and abilities against job-related criteria to identify the most qualified candidates. The federal hiring process typically includes notifying the public that the government is accepting applications for a job; screening applications against minimum qualification standards; and assessing applicants' relative competencies or knowledge, skills, and abilities against job-

---

[8]See, for example, GAO, *Human Capital: Key Principles for Effective Strategic Workforce Planning*, GAO-04-39 (Washington, D.C.: Dec. 11, 2003); Government Performance and Results Act (GPRA) (Pub. L. No. 103-62, 107. Stat 285 (1993)); and Project Management Institute, *The Standard for Program Management*, Third Edition © (Newtown Square, Pennsylvania: 2013). GAO-04-39 addresses key strategic workforce planning principles for aligning an organization's human capital program with its current and emerging mission and programmatic goals, and developing long-term strategies for acquiring, developing, and retaining staff to achieve programmatic goals. GPRA was enacted to— among other things—improve federal program effectiveness, accountability, and service delivery, in part through requiring performance plans with goals that establish target levels of performance against which achievement can be compared. While the practices called for through GPRA are required at the federal department/agency level, we have previously reported that they can serve as leading practices for planning at lower levels within federal agencies, such as individual programs or initiatives. For example, see GAO, *Foreign Aid Reform: Comprehensive Strategy, Interagency Coordination, and Operational Improvements Would Bolster Current Efforts*, GAO-09-192 (Washington, D.C.: Apr. 17, 2009). *The Standard for Program Management* outlines supporting processes for program management, including program cost budgeting and estimation.

related criteria to identify the most qualified applicants. Federal civil service employees, other than those in the Senior Executive Service, are employed in either the competitive service or the excepted service.[9] The majority of the federal civilian workforce obtains positions through the open competitive service examination process, which is intended to ensure that hiring complies with merit principles. Applicants for competitive service positions generally compete against one another through the competitive examination process.

Federal agencies follow similar processes of identifying and selecting the most qualified candidates. This process generally includes, among other things, rating and ranking candidates and preparing ranked lists of the best-qualified candidates; selecting candidates to interview; conducting reference checks and applying veterans' preference criteria; and making job offers, including conducting any preemployment checks (such as medical examinations) and security clearance checks. However, variation in how this process is carried out may occur across the four DHS components selected for our review. For example, TSA hires for all occupations as a member of the excepted service, while NPPD, USCIS, and USSS are part of the federal competitive service, though NPPD and USSS also hire for certain positions under excepted service appointing authorities. Specific to TSA, under the Aviation and Transportation Security Act, TSA is generally exempt from the provisions of Title 5 of the U.S. Code as well as the policies and procedures OPM established under Title 5, in order to adapt hiring processes to align with the unique demands of the agency's workforce.[10] Thus, TSA may adapt hiring processes as needed to meet agency needs, and has established its own hiring flexibilities. For example, TSA has an approved interchange agreement from OPM to allow permanent TSA employees to apply and be selected for vacancies in competitive service agencies.

---

[9]5 U.S.C. §§ 2102(a), 2103(a). Only certain positions are in the excepted service and are excepted from the competitive examination process. Positions may be excepted from the competitive service by statute, by the President, or by OPM. 5 C.F.R. § 213.101. OPM may except positions from the competitive service when it determines that appointments into such positions through competitive examination are not practicable. 5 C.F.R. § 6.1(a). Excepted appointments can be under either Schedule A (e.g., chaplain and attorney positions), Schedule B (e.g., Student Career Experience Program and Senior Executive Service candidate development program positions), or Schedule C (e.g., political appointee positions). 5 C.F.R. Part 213, Subpart C.

[10]49 U.S.C. § 114(n), 49 U.S.C. § 40122(g).

DHS Recruiting and Hiring Roles and Responsibilities

Within DHS, OCHCO is responsible for ensuring that DHS has the programs, policies, processes, and resources to recruit, hire, train, and retain its overall workforce. OCHCO's strategic human capital agenda includes, among other things, recruiting a diverse workforce, hiring veterans, and improving the hiring process. Within OCHCO, specifically with respect to recruiting, D&I focuses on coordinating and leveraging component resources to achieve departmental recruiting and outreach goals, which are to reduce recruiting costs, increase efficiencies, and increase the diversity of applicant pools. While D&I administers human resource services related to recruiting and hiring for DHS headquarters, individual DHS components are primarily responsible for the active recruiting and hiring of employees for their components—that is, identifying their own occupational needs, including monitoring workforce data on grade, seniority, demographics, and attrition rates. Individual components also have their own recruiting and hiring budgets and are responsible for reaching out to potential applicants through job fairs, recruiting events, and other marketing efforts. Individual components manage their own application and hiring processes, including evaluation of potential candidates through selection.

OCHCO human capital programs and initiatives are supported, developed, and implemented through various cross-component councils, as well as implementation of DHS strategic human capital goals and priorities. For example, in May 2010, as part of its role in facilitating department-wide recruiting efforts, D&I led the development of the Corporate Recruiting Council (CRC), which holds monthly meetings with recruitment officers from DHS components as a means to encourage coordination and sharing of recruiting and hiring practices and strategies. CRC is chaired by D&I and has representatives from all of DHS's components. Through the CRC, D&I focuses on presenting a "one DHS" image by serving as the focal point for department-wide recruitment procedures and guidance, leveraging resources, and facilitating coordination and information sharing among components on recruiting events, best practices, and strategies.

Recruiting and Hiring as an Element of Strategic Workforce Planning

We have previously reported on the importance of strategic workforce planning and focusing on developing long-term strategies for acquiring, developing, and retaining an organization's total workforce.[11] Strategic workforce planning includes the determination of critical skills and competencies—such as the identification of MCOs—to meet both current and future programmatic needs and developing strategies tailored to address gaps in the number, skills, competencies, and deployment of the workforce.[12] DHS has developed and, in November 2012, updated a workforce planning guide that provides steps, tools, and resources that components are to use to plan for current and future organizational and workforce needs. One key element of strategic workforce planning is recruiting and hiring, which is intended to identify and acquire employees with the necessary skills and competencies to meet agency programmatic needs.[13] In December 2012, we reported on strategic workforce planning efforts at DHS—specifically, that while DHS had taken steps that are generally consistent with leading principles in managing departmental strategic workforce planning, OCHCO had made limited progress in developing an oversight approach for monitoring and evaluating component-level efforts.[14] To provide a basis for monitoring and assessment of department-wide workforce planning efforts, we recommended that DHS identify and document additional performance

---

[11]GAO-04-39.

[12]As we reported in September 2012, OPM and the Chief Human Capital Officers Council (a body composed of chief human capital officers of 24 executive agencies, chaired by OPM, to advise and assist the head of the agency and other agency officials in their strategic human capital efforts) established a working group in September 2011 to identify and mitigate critical skills gaps as a means to address the federal government's human capital high-risk area. See GAO, *Human Capital Management: Effectively Implementing Reforms and Closing Critical Skills Gaps Are Key to Addressing Federal Workforce Challenges*, GAO-12-1023T (Washington, D.C.: Sept. 19, 2012). In conjunction with OPM efforts to identify and mitigate skill gaps, DHS's OCHCO is overseeing a pilot project to assess competency gaps for selected MCOs at DHS.

[13]DHS's Workforce Planning Model identifies five steps for effective workforce planning—(1) set a strategic direction; (2) identify supply and demand discrepancies; (3) develop an action plan; (4) implement the action plan; and (5) monitor, evaluate, and revise. Within these five steps are 15 elements, 1 of which involves recruitment, hiring, training, and placement. See GAO, *DHS Strategic Workforce Planning: Oversight of Departmentwide Efforts Should Be Strengthened*, GAO-13-65 (Washington, D.C.: Dec. 3, 2012). In addition to recruiting and hiring, training is also a key element in the workforce planning model and can help address skill and competency gaps. We have ongoing work examining training programs at DHS and plan to report the results of our review in 2014.

[14]GAO-13-65.

measures, document policies and procedures to use the results of audits related to component-level workforce planning, and integrate the results of these audits with components' annual operational plans and review these plans. DHS concurred with these recommendations and has reported taking steps to address them, but they are not yet fully implemented.

In 2011, at the direction of OCHCO, DHS's components identified their MCOs. OCHCO validated that these MCOs represent those jobs that are most critical to accomplishment of the mission, rather than simply the jobs that are most populous within each component (although some MCOs are the most populous within a component). For example, USCIS's sole MCO is the immigration services officer (ISO) position, while one of TSA's five MCOs is its transportation security officer (TSO).[15] DHS completed the process of revalidating the MCOs that represent those occupations most critical for DHS to fulfill its mission in August 2013 and plans to do so again every 2 years hereafter.[16] See appendix I for a list of all MCOs for the four components in our review.

As shown in figure 1, the size of DHS's workforce has grown in recent years and the majority of DHS's workforce is composed of MCOs.

---

[15]ISOs are responsible for the adjudication of applications and petitions for immigration benefits and privileges. TSOs implement security screening procedures to protect the traveling public by, in part, assisting in conducting screening of passengers, baggage, and cargo.

[16]According to OCHCO, the revalidated MCO list is awaiting review and approval by the Chief Human Capital Officer.

Figure 1: Total Department of Homeland Security (DHS) Employees Onboard and Mission-Critical Occupation (MCO) Employees Onboard, from Fiscal Years 2008-2012

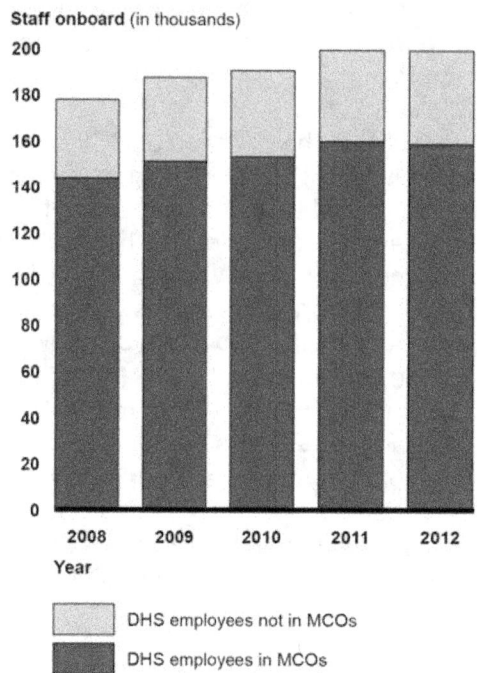

Staff onboard (in thousands)

☐ DHS employees not in MCOs

■ DHS employees in MCOs

Source: GAO analysis of Enterprise Human Resource Integration data.

Note: The total DHS employee count does not include U.S. Coast Guard military members or DHS employees in intelligence-related positions. According to DHS, these groups account for approximately 40,000 additional staff.

This figure represents all occupational series that contain MCOs. In some instances, MCO positions are subsets of the occupational series that cannot be identified more granularly (e.g., cybersecurity personnel are a subset of information technology [IT] specialists). Thus, this figure likely overstates the true proportion of MCOs within DHS.

Our High-Risk Work Related to DHS Recruiting and Hiring Efforts

In January 2003, we designated implementing and transforming DHS as a high-risk area because DHS had to transform 22 existing agencies—several with major management challenges—into one department. Human capital—including recruiting and hiring efforts—is among the challenges we have identified that DHS faces in implementing and transforming itself. To address this high-risk designation, DHS needs to achieve 31 specific actions and outcomes, 1 of which is related to recruiting and hiring. These actions and outcomes are based on the issues we have identified and recommendations made through our work at DHS.

In January 2011, DHS issued its initial *Integrated Strategy for High Risk Management*, which included key management initiatives (e.g., Workforce Strategy, Workforce Planning and Balanced Workforce, and Outreach and Targeted Recruitment) and corrective actions to address these high-risk areas as well as the actions and outcomes we identified as needed to address the high-risk designation. DHS agreed with these actions and outcomes and designated senior DHS officials to be responsible for implementing them. DHS provided updates of its progress in implementing these initiatives, including recruiting and hiring, in later versions of the strategy in June 2011, December 2011, and June 2012. In its September 2012 update to the June 2012 *Integrated Strategy for High Risk Management*, describing DHS's progress in implementing a recruiting and hiring strategy that is targeted to fill both short- and long-term needs, and specifically to fill identified human capital gaps, including diversity and foreign language gaps, DHS reported that it has partially addressed this outcome, which we validated in December 2012.[17] In our most recent high-risk update, in February 2013, we reported that DHS needs to continue to demonstrate sustained progress in addressing this outcome.[18] In its June 2013 update, DHS reported that it has now mostly addressed this outcome.[19] We are continuing to evaluate the

---

[17] In reporting on progress in addressing high-risk outcomes, GAO and DHS generally use the following nomenclature: fully addressed = outcome is fully addressed; mostly addressed = progress is significant and a small amount of work remains; partially addressed = progress is measurable, but significant work remains; and initiated = activities have been initiated to address outcome, but it is too early to report progress.

[18] GAO, *High-Risk Series: An Update*, GAO-13-283 (Washington, D.C.: February 2013).

[19] DHS, *Integrated Strategy for High Risk Management* (Washington, D.C.: June 27, 2013).

appropriateness of this designation as part of our ongoing high-risk work, and plan to use the results from this report to inform our own evaluations of this outcome in our future high-risk updates.

DHS and Selected Components Are Implementing Recruiting and Hiring Strategies to Fill Mission-Critical Occupations

DHS has developed and taken steps to implement a coordinated recruiting and outreach strategy and address resource constraints. In addition, the four components we selected for review have various efforts under way to develop and implement their own targeted recruiting and hiring strategies. Components reported that they have generally been successful in filling MCOs.

DHS Has Developed and Taken Steps to Implement a Coordinated Recruiting and Outreach Strategy and Address Budgetary Constraints

While DHS components are largely responsible for specific activities and efforts to recruit and hire for their MCOs, DHS has taken steps to help ensure greater coordination and resource sharing among components. Specifically, in 2011, D&I—through the CRC—developed the CROS to better coordinate and link component recruiting and outreach efforts to hiring for DHS mission and workforce needs (for all positions, including MCOs), and leverage resources as well as reduce recruiting costs, among other things. The CROS provides a high-level strategy that supports DHS's goal from its Workforce Strategy for Fiscal Years 2011-2016 to "recruit a highly qualified and diverse workforce." It is designed to, among other things, guide outreach and recruitment efforts across DHS, leverage all outreach and recruiting resources, and integrate recruiting and outreach plans across DHS.

According to D&I officials, the CROS was largely developed to help relieve some of the fragmentation of component recruitment efforts, reflecting a recent DHS-wide emphasis on having components work together to present an image of "one DHS"—rather than individual components—to potential applicants at outreach events.[20] One means of doing this is by having components coordinate to share booth space under the DHS banner at recruiting events. For example, if USSS and TSA are both hoping to hire law enforcement officers, they might agree to share the registration fee at a recruiting event (or take turns paying fees at alternate events) and have staff from each component together at one table to speak to potential applicants about their respective positions. D&I officials state that this sharing of resources is important to the department, as devoting additional resources to increasing overall recruiting efforts has not been a high priority for DHS over the past year, given budget constraints. Other D&I efforts to implement the CROS across DHS are shown in table 1.

---

[20]According to D&I, this "one DHS" vision was widely communicated to the department's components via a memo from the Secretary of Homeland Security announcing DHS's Workforce Strategy in December 2010. In particular, the Secretary stated that "the time for fragmented, duplicative, and sometimes competing branding and recruitment is over," and called for development of a coordinated recruitment strategy presenting a unified image of DHS.

Table 1: Office of Diversity and Inclusion (D&I) Efforts to Implement the *Coordinated Recruiting and Outreach Strategy* (CROS)

Effort	Description
Component Specific Outreach and Recruiting Plan (CSORP)	Beginning in 2012, D&I began directing components to develop CSORPs that align with the CROS. The CSORPs are component-level plans developed annually and intended to cover a 5-year period, with a focus on veterans and diversity outreach efforts, to help components identify and organize their focus in recruiting efforts.[a] CSORPs are also intended to provide D&I—which reviews the reports annually—with greater ability to monitor components' plans to link recruiting efforts with mission-critical occupation (MCO) hiring needs. Components in our review generally developed these CSORPs, but three of the four plans we reviewed did not include all the directed elements (e.g., MCO hiring needs, veterans targets, outreach efforts by population, and planned recruiting and outreach expenditures).[b]
"Top 25" list of recruitment events	In 2012, D&I, working with components through the Corporate Recruiting Council (CRC), established a "Top 25" list of recruitment events that components have identified as having large pools of diverse applicants.[c] D&I encourages components to partner to attend these events and touts development of this list as an important effort of the CRC.
Shared database on recruiting events	In 2012, D&I implemented a shared database that allows components to report information on recruiting events (e.g., costs, key population groups recruited, approximate number of attendees) in an attempt to gather consistent information from components on recruiting events.
MCO Onboard Diversity Snapshots	On a quarterly basis, D&I reviews "MCO onboard diversity snapshots," which present data on current levels of employment by race/ethnicity and gender, focused on law enforcement officer (LEO) and LEO-related positions. D&I considers LEO and LEO-related positions the priority MCOs for DHS, since D&I stated these represent the majority of all MCO positions. Thus, these positions have been the focus of D&I's review of component efforts to fill MCOs. These data provide D&I leadership with information on how the components are doing in staffing these positions for each of these applicant groups, as well as opportunities to potentially increase outreach to groups they may consider underrepresented.

Source: GAO analysis of DHS information.

[a] In general, CSORPs are expected to identify each component's key recruiting and outreach officials; annual veterans and disabled veterans hiring targets for 5 years; MCOs targeted for recruitment; plans for recruiting and outreach by race, ethnicity, and gender (i.e., underrepresented groups as identified by components); and estimated recruiting and outreach costs. This aligns with DHS's department-wide emphasis on increased hiring of veterans and other diversity populations.

[b] For example, while USSS provided all requested items in its fiscal years 2012 through 2016 CSORP, USCIS, TSA, and NPPD did not provide 5-year veterans hiring targets in the CSORP (though D&I reports that all components do provide OCHCO with annual reports discussing their efforts to recruit veterans and meet annual veteran hiring targets). D&I officials informed us that in their first year of reviewing CSORPs, they were less concerned with whether the components provided every element called for in the D&I-provided template than if the plans identified key MCO hiring needs and the components' outreach efforts to find applicants to meet those needs.

[c] Examples include conferences and job fairs held by associations such as the National Native American Law Enforcement Association, National Organization of Black Law Enforcement Executives, Hispanic American Police Command Officer Association, and Women in Federal Law Enforcement.

D&I officials have emphasized that their role is to assist components in coordinating and linking recruiting efforts, ensure that component recruiting efforts are tied to filling MCOs, and review high-level data on diversity employment in DHS, rather than explicitly telling components how they should go about recruiting and hiring for positions. D&I officials said they have fulfilled their role by developing and implementing the CROS and facilitating components' efforts to coordinate and share effective recruiting practices through the CRC. Officials from all four components we interviewed generally spoke well of the CRC as a helpful vehicle for sharing information on recruiting and hiring among components and coordinating recruiting efforts when feasible, and on the role of D&I in facilitating recruiting and hiring efforts. While component officials noted that they support in concept DHS efforts to coordinate recruiting, officials from two of the four components we interviewed voiced concerns that the efforts to have components represent themselves simply as DHS entities—or have representatives from other components speak to potential job applicants on their behalf—could make it difficult for some components to communicate the unique aspects of their missions and occupations. D&I officials stated that it is not DHS's intent to take away components' identities, but to encourage collaboration, and that they have gotten positive feedback on these efforts from components in the field.

While D&I has taken steps to implement the CROS across DHS, D&I has been limited in its ability to implement some elements, largely because of budget constraints, according to D&I officials. For example, in accordance with a CROS objective to coordinate recruitment planning procedures to reduce duplication of effort and travel costs, D&I planned to roll out "one DHS" training for component recruiters at five regional sites to encourage coordinated and shared recruiting efforts at the field level. However, D&I suspended this effort after training at the first two sites because of budgetary constraints, and has not determined when the budget will allow it to continue the training efforts. In the meantime, D&I is considering hosting webcasts or video teleconferences to train recruiting officials in the field who may be interested in learning about other components. In addition, the CROS calls for an annual marketing plan and process to centralize recruiting-related advertising to create a unified image of DHS to job seekers. However, according to D&I officials, budgetary constraints have also placed this work on hold.

Selected Components Have Implemented Various Recruiting and Hiring Strategies and Efforts

In addition to preparing CSORPs, the four components we selected for review have various efforts under way to develop and implement their own targeted recruiting and hiring strategies. For example, all components generally reported forming relationships with and targeting colleges and universities, and attending recruiting events that serve veterans and diverse populations (e.g., Women in Federal Law Enforcement and the Wounded Warriors Program). While not required by OCHCO, components may develop their own specific targeted recruitment strategies to guide their efforts in identifying the best possible candidates for their unique missions and occupational requirements. For example, as explained in table 2, TSA and USSS have developed targeted recruiting strategies, while USCIS has elected not to develop such a strategy, and NPPD plans to develop one in the future.

Table 2: Recruiting Strategies of Selected Components in Our Review

Component	Strategy/approach to recruiting
Transportation Security Administration (TSA)	TSA has an overall strategic recruitment plan for its transportation security officers (TSO) agency-wide.[a] TSA has also developed a number of more targeted plans aimed at recruiting TSOs (and personnel for other positions) for specific airports. For example, in 2010 TSA developed a recruiting strategy specifically for TSOs at an airport in the southeastern United States. This strategy identified target populations for recruiting (e.g., members of the military), outreach organizations, and local publications and marketing events in the area that could be used to better "brand" TSA for potential applicants. According to TSA officials, these types of targeted recruiting strategies help them to take into account area workforce demographics; specific airport needs (e.g., more female TSOs); and specific recruitment events and outreach organizations, which could increase the likelihood that the component can register and track the success of particular recruiting and outreach efforts stemming from each recruiting strategy. In addition, TSA has a strategy specific to veterans' recruiting.
United States Secret Service (USSS)	USSS produces an annual recruiting and outreach plan that contains projected staffing targets for key occupations and a number of goals, activities, and performance measures based largely on levels of outreach (e.g., attend a certain number of events for military and diversity groups; advertise via brochures and electronic newsletters; and conduct employment information sessions with educational institutions, professional organizations, and the public). While efforts to implement this plan are not directly tied to hiring specific numbers of employees, they provide USSS with a road map for increasing outreach to certain diversity areas. In addition, USSS prepares annual recruitment accomplishment reports that provide details on the number and types of recruitment events attended during the fiscal year—broken out by target populations—as well as estimated cost savings through reduced registration fees.[b] For example, USSS reported attending 691 recruiting events in fiscal year 2012 targeting a number of populations.
United States Citizenship and Immigration Services (USCIS)	USCIS does not have a component-level targeted recruiting and outreach strategy. According to USCIS officials, it does not have any problems attracting sufficient numbers of applicants to fill its immigration services officer (ISO) slots—its sole mission-critical occupation (MCO).[c] There are needs for ISOs with different skill sets in different offices and regions of the nation, officials said, so a national "one size fits all" recruiting strategy would not be optimal for them. Officials added that they may consider developing such a strategy once USCIS has completed ongoing efforts to refine its workforce planning efforts and staffing allocation model. In the meantime, much of USCIS's recruiting efforts have focused on veterans' outreach events.
National Protection and Programs Directorate (NPPD)	NPPD has not developed a component-level recruiting strategy, or a human capital strategy, because—following its human resource authority designation in 2009—recent efforts have been focused on creating its directorate-level strategic plan. NPPD officials stated that they plan to develop a human capital strategic plan—to include a recruiting and hiring strategy—pending approval of resources for fiscal year 2014. Officials report a number of ongoing efforts, such as use of special hiring authorities, to improve recruiting and hiring among cybersecurity personnel and Federal Protective Service (FPS) officers—two key MCOs.[d]

Source: GAO analysis of DHS information.

[a]TSOs— the MCO that represents TSA's most populous occupation—perform all security functions related to the screening of people, property, and cargo through the use and application of procedures, techniques, and technology.

[b]According to the 2012 recruitment accomplishment report, USSS estimates savings of approximately $35,000 in fiscal year 2012. USSS also states that despite an 85 percent cut in recruitment budget for 2012, it cut back on the number of events by 12 percent compared with the number of events for 2011. It was able to do this by, among other things, focusing on outreach through no-cost information sessions at colleges, high schools, and military installations, and providing tours to potential applicants at its headquarters and training center.

[c]USCIS has one MCO—the ISO subset within the1801 series (General Inspection, Investigation, & Compliance)—which includes field and service operations, call centers, refugee and asylum officers, and fraud detection and national security officers. According to USCIS officials, ISOs constitute over 44 percent of its workforce.

[d]FPS officers include sworn law enforcement officers and trained security experts who provide security assessments, inspections, and oversight for contract guards, and respond to crimes in progress.

In addition to their recruiting and outreach efforts, components in our review have taken steps to streamline the hiring process and reduce the time-to-hire.[21] We have reported in the past that time-consuming and paperwork-intensive processes pose challenges to recruiting and hiring in the federal government.[22] As part of larger federal hiring reforms to address this and other issues, DHS components track time-to-hire for certain MCOs and commonly filled positions.[23] According to OCHCO, components are directed by DHS to report these data to OCHCO on a quarterly basis, and OCHCO gathers and reports the time-to-hire data to OPM. OPM has established a time-to-hire target of 80 days for all federal agencies. DHS component officials generally state that they have been challenged in meeting OPM targets, and officials from two components said that it may not be possible to meet the 80-day OPM target because of the many steps involved in their hiring process. For example, many DHS positions require extensive background checks, and some require security clearances, which lengthen the time it takes to bring someone onboard. USCIS, for example, reports that in the fourth quarter of fiscal year 2012, its average time to hire ISOs was 117 days. However, USCIS officials stated that they did not believe this time frame was driving candidates away from seeking positions, adding that they rarely make job offers that are not accepted. In addition, components are studying their time-to-hire data and seeking ways to reduce this time in an effort to meet OPM targets. TSA reports that it has been able to reduce time-to-hire for its management, administrative, and professional positions from an average of approximately 112 days to 104 days between the first and second quarters of fiscal year 2013 and is exploring efforts to further streamline the hiring process, such as developing a standard job announcement.[24] TSA is also working to reduce time-to-hire for its TSOs

---

[21]"Time-to-hire" is a measure of the amount of time taken to bring an employee onboard, from the date a new hire action is authorized through the date a new employee begins working.

[22]GAO-08-762T.

[23]A presidential memorandum dated May 11, 2010, called on federal agencies to overhaul the way they recruit and hire the civilian workforce to, among other things, improve the ability to select high-quality candidates efficiently and quickly. The memorandum also directed federal agencies to report on and attempt to reduce time-to-hire for mission-critical and commonly filled occupations. Memorandum, Improving the Federal Recruitment and Hiring Process, 75 Fed. Reg. 27,157 (May 11, 2010).

[24]TSA's management, professional, and administrative positions cover all employees except for TSOs, entry-level federal air marshals, and Senior Executive Service.

GAO-13-742 DHS Recruiting and Hiring

by working closely with airport hiring officials to determine the appropriate size of their "ready pool" for hiring.[25] USSS also reported making efforts to reduce time-to-hire by moving more quickly to complete qualification exams and reviews of those results.

Selected Components Have Generally Been Successful in Filling MCOs

Components in our review have generally been successful in filling MCOs, in part because of the various strategies and efforts discussed above, as well as less attrition of current MCO employees, with the exception of cybersecurity personnel. Component officials stated that in assessing the state of their MCO workforces, they regularly review varied workforce data—such as hires, losses, and vacancy rates—and meet with hiring officials from their program offices to determine how well specific occupational needs are being met or what challenges may be affecting them.[26] It is important to note that there are multiple indicators that agencies can use to determine the health of their workforces and their success in filling MCOs and other positions. We present data on hires, losses, and vacancy rates, when available, because these are indicators that the selected components use to assess their workforce health and to identify recruiting and hiring needs.[27]

---

[25] The ready pool refers to TSO candidates who have passed all assessments, including background and medical checks, and are eligible to receive a job offer from the airport(s) to which they applied, which helps to ensure that qualified candidates are available for hire at all times. Once job opportunity announcements are posted, candidates are then processed through each of the subsequent assessment steps as the airports' hiring needs dictate. TSA tracks time-to-hire for its TSO positions in two different manners. As reported to OPM through OCHCO, time-to-hire consists of the time taken for an airport to formally open a position for hiring until a new hire is brought on board (or, the time taken to move an applicant from the ready pool to onboard status). As of March 2013, this average time-to-hire was 37 days for TSOs. However, to better capture the "end to end" time to hire TSOs, TSA also internally tracks the average amount of time elapsed between a new hire's submission of an application until he or she is brought on board. This average time-to-hire is approximately 150 days. TSA officials explained that this time frame is greatly affected by the length of time an applicant may have to wait between filling out an initial application and reporting to TSA for further assessments, which in turn is affected by the hiring needs of that applicant's airport of choice.

[26] For the purposes of this report, "losses" refer to employees that have left a component because of resignation, retirement, or other separation from the component.

[27] There are a number of factors and events that can influence vacancy rates at various points in time and for variable durations, including changes in staffing allocations, attrition of staff, budget factors, and changes in hiring processes—and vacancy rates fluctuate throughout the year. There is also no generally agreed-upon standard for acceptable vacancy rates.

TSA. TSA has generally been successful in recruiting and hiring for its MCOs, including TSOs, as illustrated by table 3 (which shows hiring outpacing losses over the last 3 fiscal years) and comments from TSA officials.[28]

Table 3: Number of Hires and Losses for Transportation Security Officers (TSO), Fiscal Years 2010-2012

Fiscal year	Hires	Losses
2010	4,059	4,002
2011	8,787	4,682
2012	5,947	5,620

Source: TSA.

Note: Transportation security officers perform all security functions related to the screening of people, property, and cargo through the use and application of procedures, techniques, and technology.

TSA human capital officials stated that they assess success in hiring TSOs by reviewing data and meeting with program officials to discuss whether hiring needs at particular airports are being met. TSA produces a weekly report that captures the number of TSOs that need to be hired to meet certain airports' needed TSO allocations, as well as the number of candidates that have been certified for the ready pool. The report also contains the number of TSOs that have been brought onboard over the prior 2 months and those projected to be brought onboard the next month. When airport hiring needs are identified, TSA human capital officials said they examine the weekly report to ensure that there are enough candidates in the ready pool; if not, officials work to identify job fairs and outreach efforts in that airport's geographic area to recruit more candidates. TSA human capital officials noted that they also meet with program offices' hiring managers to get feedback on recruiting and hiring processes and challenges that may need to be addressed.

TSA human capital officials cited a number of factors that contribute to the agency's success in filling TSO positions. In particular, officials said that their development and use of hiring flexibilities has been helpful in attracting candidates for TSO positions. For example, TSA—working in

---

[28]TSA officials informed us that they generally do not track vacancy rates for positions but rely on program offices to report to them on job needs to be filled.

collaboration with OPM—has established a policy allowing part-time TSOs to purchase health insurance at the same rate as full-time employees. This is a benefit that is not available to employees hired by competitive service agencies. According to TSA officials, this flexibility has been useful in hiring TSOs because many TSOs are hired on a part-time basis.

TSA officials reported facing some challenges in hiring TSOs, particularly in certain geographic areas, such as remote areas or locations where there is greater competition for qualified candidates. As one example, TSA officials reported that in North Dakota, burgeoning oil field work offers greater pay for qualified applicants. To mitigate these challenges, officials reported using more direct e-mail and radio communications to potential job seekers, or visiting one-stop employment centers. Officials informed us that these hiring challenges have not affected TSA's ability to meet its mission as overtime pay is used to fund additional shift coverage, among other things.

USSS. USSS has generally been able to fill MCO positions. As shown in table 4, vacancy rates were generally below 3 percent for MCO positions during fiscal years 2010 through 2012.

Table 4: Number of U.S. Secret Service Hires and Losses, and Vacancy Rates for Mission-Critical Occupations (MCO), Fiscal Years 2010-2013 (as of March 2013)

Fiscal year	Data	Special agents	Uniformed Division police officers	Special officers	Protective/physical support officers	MCOs total
2010	Hires	162	205	3	4	374
	Losses	122	125	8	7	262
	Vacancy	0.25%	0.93%	N/A	N/A	0.4%
2011	Hires	91	135	4	3	233
	Losses	120	69	3	5	197
	Vacancy	0.45%	-1.43%	N/A	N/A	-0.08%
2012	Hires	0	21	8	2	31
	Losses	100	56	6	7	169
	Vacancy	2.99%	2.95%	0.74%	2.22%	2.87%
2013[a]	Hires	0	0	2	0	2
	Losses	59	27	3	3	92
	Vacancy	4.69%	4.99%	12.84%	4.26%	4.99%

Source: United States Secret Service.

Notes: Special agents are criminal investigators who investigate violations of U.S. laws, perform security surveys and background investigations, and assist U.S. Attorneys. They also ensure protection of officials and their families and perform other protective duties such as advance security surveys of domestic locations. Uniformed Division police officers provide security for physical buildings, such as the White House, Vice President's residence, designated embassies, and other specified federal property, among other things. Special officers maintain security posts, monitor and operate communications systems, and inspect and operate protective vehicles, among other things. Protective/physical support officers plan, develop, and implement a technical security program for major protective advance trips involving designated protectees, and conduct technical investigative support functions, among other things.

N/A (not available) means that USSS did not collect these data for those positions during the applicable time frame.

[a]As of March 2013.

While USSS officials stated that when funding is available, they generally have been able to fill their MCO positions; they added that funding constraints in fiscal year 2012 limited their recruiting, outreach, and hiring efforts, which led to higher vacancy rates in fiscal years 2012 and 2013 to date. For example, because of funding constraints, USSS did not hire any special agents (who conduct criminal investigations and ensure protection of officials and their families) in fiscal year 2012 or in 2013 to date, and hiring for Uniformed Division police officers (who provide protection for property such as the White House and Vice President's residence) has not kept pace with losses in fiscal year 2012 or 2013 to date, as shown in table 4. For the special agents, officials stated that while their protective mission is adequately staffed, there are now fewer man hours to support field office investigative responsibilities. However, USSS officials told us that Uniformed Division protective responsibilities have largely not been affected as USSS has reprogrammed staff from administrative and training functions, increased overtime, and reduced noncritical training.

USCIS. Data on job applications, hires, and losses—as well as discussions with USCIS officials—show that USCIS has not faced challenges hiring ISOs, who hold the only MCO position within USCIS. Specifically, USCIS officials told us they receive thousands of applicants for vacant ISO positions, and have been able to fill these vacancies without difficulty. For example, during 2012, USCIS received applications from over 27,000 minimally qualified applicants for approximately 200 ISO vacancies, and through April of fiscal year 2013, USCIS had approximately 329 ISO new hires compared with 77 losses.[29]

NPPD. NPPD has experienced some successes and challenges in filling its MCOs. As shown in table 5, NPPD's new hires have outpaced losses for all MCOs component-wide since fiscal year 2010.

Table 5: Number of New Hires and Losses for all National Protection and Programs Directorate Mission-Critical Occupations, Fiscal Years 2010-2013 (as of May 2013)

Fiscal year	Hires	Losses
2010	145	52
2011	144	69
2012	182	89
2013[a]	123	66

Source: National Protection and Programs Directorate.

Notes: These data include interns and summer hires for all NPPD MCO positions as defined in appendix I.

[a] As of May 2013.

[29]USCIS tracks and reviews vacancy rates by office (e.g., Field Operations, Service Center Operations), but does not track these rates by position (e.g., ISOs). The 27,000 minimally qualified applicants cited here were deemed minimally qualified after initial screening and prior to any screening conducted by USCIS.

Despite these component-wide successes, NPPD has recently struggled with filling some key MCOs, such as those for FPS officers and cybersecurity personnel.[30] For example, NPPD officials informed us that despite receiving a large number of applicants, FPS has faced challenges in meeting its statutorily mandated target levels for officers, which have increased in recent years.[31] As of June 2013, FPS had 955 officers onboard versus a target of 1,007 officers. While there is no specific target for vacancy rates, officials noted that they hope to meet their target level for officers onboard this fiscal year. Officials cited the rigorous and lengthy preemployment background, medical, and drug checks as a primary challenge in hiring at FPS. To mitigate this challenge, NPPD officials reported accepting a larger qualified applicant pool during the preemployment process and increasing the use of Veterans Hiring Authority and direct hire authority at job fairs, wherein FPS can make tentative job offers on the spot pending clearance of background and other checks.

As of June 2013, CS&C—the NPPD subcomponent that houses cybersecurity personnel—had a vacancy rate of 22 percent. In attempting to fill cybersecurity positions, NPPD officials reported facing some challenges because of the length of time taken to conduct security checks needed to grant Top Secret/Sensitive Compartmented Information clearances when needed, low pay in comparison with that of private sector positions, and lack of clearly defined skill sets or a unique occupational series for these positions. We have previously reported on a number of these and other related challenges in the federal cybersecurity workforce.[32] NPPD has taken a number of steps to mitigate the challenges of filling cybersecurity positions, such as using direct hire authority/flexibilities and establishing relationships with "centers of

---

[30]FPS officers are sworn law enforcement officers and trained security experts who provide security assessments, inspections, and oversight for contract guards, and respond to crimes in progress. Cybersecurity personnel are spread throughout a number of different occupational series within NPPD, but are generally concentrated in the Information Technology (2210) series. Thus, there is not a specific occupational series that houses all cybersecurity personnel, and NPPD could not provide us with hire and loss data for cybersecurity personnel alone. See GAO-12-8 for further information on the difficulties faced by federal agencies in determining the size of their cybersecurity workforce, in part because of this lack of a specific job series.

[31]See, e.g., Pub. L. No. 113-6, 127 Stat. 198, 355 (2013).

[32]See GAO-12-8.

academic excellence" to create a pipeline of qualified candidates to hire. NPPD officials also noted that there are ongoing department-wide efforts to better define and strengthen the required skill set for DHS cybersecurity personnel, including pursuit of a specific cybersecurity personnel job series, which officials expect to ultimately better inform recruiting and hiring.

D&I Is Taking Steps to Assess Implementation of the CROS, but Could Improve Tracking of Recruiting Costs

D&I has established performance measures to assess progress in implementing the goals and objectives of the CROS, and plans to develop performance targets in future iterations of the CROS to better track component performance. D&I could better measure department-wide recruiting and outreach costs by tracking recruiting costs from all DHS components in a consistent manner. In addition, DHS is taking steps to better measure return on investment for recruiting and outreach activities, a key focus of the CROS.

D&I Plans to Better Assess CROS Implementation through Performance Targets, but Could Better Measure Department wide Recruiting Costs

D&I assesses departmental and component progress in implementing the CROS by tracking and monitoring component efforts for six performance measures that are aligned with six corresponding objectives and two long-term goals (shown in table 6).

Table 6: Goals, Objectives, and Performance Measures in the *Coordinated Recruiting and Outreach Strategy* (CROS)

Goals/objectives
Goal 1: Recruit a highly qualified and diverse workforce
Objective 1.1: Establish enterprise-wide outreach and recruiting plans, ensuring links to overarching strategies and statutory requirements *Performance measure:* Percentage of Department of Homeland Security (DHS) headquarters and component recruiting and outreach portfolios fully developed *Fiscal year 2012 performance measure result:* 100 percent[a]
Objective 1.2: Standardize tracking and data reporting on recruiting, outreach, and marketing activities *Performance measure:* Percentage of DHS headquarters and components in compliance with tracking and data-reporting requirements *Fiscal year 2012 performance measure result:* 62 percent
Objective 1.3: Develop methodologies that foster the creation of focused recruitment and outreach strategies based upon workforce planning and mission-critical needs *Performance measure:* Percentage of components with data-driven targeted recruitment and outreach plans that link to organizational needs *Fiscal year 2012 performance measure result:* 100 percent[a]
Goal 2: Optimize outreach and recruiting resources enterprise-wide
Objective 2.1: Coordinate recruitment and outreach planning procedures to reduce duplication of effort and travel costs *Performance measure:* Percentage decrease in recruiting cost, by component *Fiscal year 2012 performance measure result:* $22,590 in savings in fiscal year 2012
Objective 2.2: Establish annual planning mechanisms that ensure the coordination of outreach and recruiting resources *Performance measure:* Percentage decrease in component-specific participation at outreach and recruiting events *Fiscal year 2012 performance measure result:* Office of Diversity and Inclusion (D&I) is revisiting this objective and its milestones because of the changing budget environment
Objective 2.3: Establish a planning framework to create a unified image of DHS to applicants and job seekers, maintaining DHS branding guidelines *Performance measure:* Percentage increase in booth sharing and shared advertising *Fiscal year 2012 performance measure result:* Deferring until 2014 because of budgetary constraints

Source: DHS *Coordinated Recruiting and Outreach Strategy* (CROS).

[a]D&I officials reported that 100 percent compliance in these measures was achieved through component preparation of Component Specific Outreach and Recruiting Plans (CSORP). However, as we noted earlier, not all components provided all elements called for in D&I's CSORP template. The officials reported that their reviews of CSORPs were more subjective and focused on whether the components identified mission-critical occupation (MCO) hiring needs and efforts planned to meet those needs.

While these measures are aligned with and cover key aspects of performance related to the goals and objectives outlined in the CROS, they do not include performance targets to track long-term, short-term, or interim component progress toward achieving the goals of the CROS over the period the strategy covers (2012–2017). As shown in table 6, all six measures in the CROS use percentages to quantitatively indicate the extent to which the measure is being achieved. However, none of these measures identify a target percentage, or standard, against which to assess component performance. For example, the performance measure for objective 2.2 calls for a percentage decrease in component-specific participation at recruiting events, but it does not identify any target percentages to assess component performance in achieving the measure or goal 2 in the CROS, which is to optimize outreach and recruiting resources enterprise-wide. In addition, one of the measures (1.1) calls for components to have fully developed recruiting and outreach portfolios, which the CROS defines as including both short- and long-term workforce plans, strategic and tactical plans, and diversity snapshots. While D&I officials indicated that all components have fully developed recruiting and outreach portfolios—which D&I views as the CSORPs—the CSORPs do not uniformly include long-term planning as defined in the CROS (3 to 5 years). More specifically, CSORPs for the four components in our review focused on current-year efforts to reach out to underrepresented populations, and one contained a target for long-term veterans hiring. D&I revised the CSORP development template for fiscal year 2013 to focus on current-year efforts and did not request that components include long-term goals or targets in their CSORPs. Officials stated that they made this change to gather more baseline data before focusing on longer-term goals.

A performance measure should tell an organization how well it is achieving its goals, and GPRA defines a performance goal as a target level of performance expressed as a tangible, measurable objective, against which actual achievement can be compared, including a goal expressed as a quantitative standard, value, or rate.[33] In addition, both

---

[33]Pub. L. No. 103-62, 107 Stat. 285 (1993). GPRA was intended to address several broad purposes, including strengthening the confidence of the American people in their government; improving federal program effectiveness, accountability, and service delivery; and enhancing congressional decision making by providing more objective information on program performance. GPRA requires agencies to establish goals and targets to define the level of performance to be achieved by a program and express such goals in an objective, quantifiable, and measurable form. If an agency, in consultation with the Office of Management and Budget, determines that it is not feasible to express performance goals in an objective, quantifiable, and measurable form, an alternative form may be authorized. This alternative form should include separate descriptive statements of a minimally effective program and a successful program, or an alternative that would allow for an accurate independent determination of whether the program activity's performance meets the criteria of the description; or state why it is infeasible to express a performance goal in any form. 31 U.S.C. § 1115(c).

the CROS and our prior work highlight the need for recruiting and outreach strategies to be linked directly to short- and long-range plans, and our prior work has also stated that measures, such as outputs or intermediate outcomes, can be used to show progress or contribution to intended results.[34]

D&I officials stated that they and the components are in the early stages of implementing and assessing the CROS and are continuing to obtain performance data to establish a baseline level of performance for the six measures they have, including assessing the extent to which the measures themselves are appropriate and identifying the necessary actions and activities required to achieve their long-term goals. Given this, and the uncertainty associated with current federal budget and hiring constraints, D&I officials said that they felt it was premature to call for the CROS and CSORPs to identify short-term, interim, or long-term targets associated with their performance measures. However, D&I officials said they recognize the need to establish clearer links in the CROS between the actions being taken and the extent to which they are helping DHS and the components achieve the long-term goals of the CROS, in part by developing targets for measures. D&I officials told us they plan to address these issues in future updates to the CROS. Taking steps to update the CROS to include performance targets to measure and link component efforts with a desired set of outcomes is an important step to help clarify the ultimate desired outcomes of DHS's recruiting and outreach strategy and the specific actions DHS and components need to take on a short-term or interim basis to achieve the long-term goals outlined in the CROS.

In addition, one of the objectives in the CROS (2.1) is to coordinate recruitment and outreach planning procedures to reduce duplication of effort and travel costs. D&I has developed a database for components to use to track recruiting and outreach efforts and costs, but it does not require that all components use this database or enter data in a consistent manner. As a result, D&I does not have the information required to accurately assess component performance for this objective. D&I officials said that since many components have their own systems for

---

[34]GAO, *Agency Performance Plans: Examples of Practices That Can Improve Usefulness to Decisionmakers*, GAO/GGD/AIMD-99-69 (Washington, D.C.: Feb. 26, 1999). This report illustrates how agency performance plans can better articulate a results orientation by using intermediate goals and measures to show progress or contribution to intended results, among other things.

tracking the costs associated with recruiting outreach activities (e.g., events attended, occupations for which they are recruiting, and number of attendees), they do not want the components to duplicate efforts by having them enter the same type of information in the DHS shared database. D&I officials reported that components saved approximately $22,590 in fiscal year 2012 by sharing booth space at recruiting events coordinated through the CRC. However, D&I is unaware of the total costs of all recruiting and outreach activities department-wide, and D&I officials said this amount does not represent any savings from events or activities that may have been coordinated outside of the CRC. The CROS states that "consistent tracking and reporting of recruiting and marketing data will assist DHS and its components in informed decision-making and the development of resource allocation plans for strategic outreach, recruiting and marketing activities each fiscal year," and one of its objectives calls for standardized tracking and data reporting of recruiting and outreach activities. *The Standard for Program Management* calls for an identification of program financial sources and resources, including the establishment of baseline costs as a primary financial target programs can be measured against.[35]

D&I officials said they are revisiting the usefulness of the shared database versus the time and resources spent by components to enter data, and are also considering other options for obtaining this cost information from components, including development of a template components could fill out and provide back to D&I. D&I officials acknowledged that obtaining comprehensive and consistent cost information from all components in a manner that will ensure consistent and complete reporting of such data would be a worthwhile endeavor, but officials have not determined whether and how they will do so. As a result, D&I does not have a baseline of all recruiting costs from which to measure ongoing cost savings, making it difficult to determine how well department resources are being leveraged through component coordination or assess the extent to which they are achieving the second goal of the CROS of optimizing outreach and recruiting resources department-wide. Requiring all components to provide recruiting cost information in a consistent manner would enable D&I to better track overall recruiting costs, which would help it to assess the extent to which recruiting costs are being reduced by components as a result of

---

[35]Project Management Institute, *The Standard for Program Management.*

increased coordination and leveraging resources, as called for in the CROS.

DHS Is Taking Steps to Address Challenges in Determining Return on Investment for Recruiting and Outreach Activities

The CROS discusses the importance of establishing return on investment for recruiting and outreach events.[36] According to D&I and all component officials we interviewed, tracking return on investment has primarily been the responsibility of each component, and has generally been conducted informally. D&I officials said that determining return on investment for their recruiting and outreach activities can be challenging. For example, D&I officials said information provided by candidates or new hires at recruiting events or during the hiring process is voluntary, which makes it difficult to reliably determine the reasons an individual was interested in DHS or became an employee. Nevertheless, components in our review have taken steps to better determine return on investment for recruiting and outreach events. For example, three of the four components prepare and review after-action reports to identify events that led to interaction with promising candidates.

D&I officials said that OPM is working with departments within the federal government to compile applicant data to help better link applicants and new hires to various recruiting and outreach efforts, which D&I officials said could help them better determine their return on investment for various recruiting and outreach events. D&I officials told us they anticipate obtaining data later this calendar year, noting that the data would provide information on each candidate through the entire hiring cycle from initial application up to selection. D&I officials told us that officials from other departments said that they believe the response rate will be about 40 to 50 percent. While this response rate would not represent all or most new hires, D&I officials said analysis of this information could help them better understand the nature of the applicants it is getting, including new hires that resulted from specific recruiting events or the percentage of new hires that came from colleges and universities it visited or targeted. This type of information could assist D&I in making more informed decisions in the future about where to spend limited funds on recruitment and outreach efforts.

---

[36]To calculate return on investment, the benefit (return) of an investment is divided by the cost of the investment; the result is expressed as a percentage or a ratio.

Conclusions

As DHS faces increasingly complex national security challenges, it is important that it effectively recruit and hire employees with the appropriate skills to meet its mission requirements. In recent years, we and others have identified challenges to recruiting and hiring in the federal government in general and within DHS in particular. While DHS and selected components are implementing strategies to fill MCOs, and generally report that they are able to fill MCO positions, DHS could better assess its efforts to implement the CROS and achieve recruiting cost savings by requiring all components to provide recruiting cost information in a consistent manner. Doing so would help DHS better track the amount of resources being spent on recruiting and outreach throughout DHS and assess the extent to which increased coordination and leveraging resources have decreased recruiting costs.

Recommendation for Executive Action

To help ensure that DHS has comprehensive data to help track recruiting costs and coordinated efforts, we recommend that the Secretary of Homeland Security direct OCHCO to take the following action:

- require all components to provide D&I with recruiting cost information in a consistent manner to allow better tracking of overall recruiting costs and use this information to assess the extent to which recruiting costs are being reduced by components as a result of increased coordination and leveraging resources as called for in the CROS.

Agency Comments and Our Evaluation

We provided a draft of this report to DHS for review and comment. On September 9, 2013, DHS provided written comments, which are reprinted in appendix II, and provided technical comments, which we incorporated as appropriate. DHS concurred with our recommendation and described actions planned to address it. Specifically, DHS stated that through the CRC, DHS will develop and implement a system to consistently track and analyze overall recruiting costs by all components. This information could help DHS assess the degree to which recruiting costs are being reduced through component coordination—as called for in the CROS. DHS expects to complete this effort by December 31, 2013. If fully implemented, DHS's planned actions will address the intent of this recommendation.

We are sending copies of this report to the Secretary of Homeland Security, appropriate congressional committees, and other interested parties. This report is also available at no charge on the GAO website at http://www.gao.gov.

If you or your staff have any questions about this report, please contact me at (202) 512-9627 or maurerd@gao.gov. Contact points for our Offices of Congressional Relations and Public Affairs may be found on the last page of this report. Key contributors to this report are listed in appendix III.

David C. Maurer
Director
Homeland Security and Justice Issues

List of Requesters

The Honorable Thomas R. Carper
Chairman
The Honorable Tom Coburn, MD
Ranking Member
Committee on Homeland Security and Governmental Affairs
United States Senate

The Honorable Claire McCaskill
Chair
Subcommittee on Financial and Contracting Oversight
Committee on Homeland Security and Governmental Affairs
United States Senate

The Honorable Jeff Duncan
Chairman
Subcommittee on Oversight and Management Efficiency
Committee on Homeland Security
House of Representatives

Appendix I: Mission-Critical Occupations for Selected Department of Homeland Security Components

Table 7 presents the occupational series and positions considered to be mission-critical occupations for the components in our review.

Table 7: Mission-Critical Occupations (MCO) for the Four Components in Our Review

Component	Series	Occupation	MCO Job description
National Protection and Programs Directorate (NPPD)	80	Security Administration	Security specialist (NPPD-wide): analyzes; interprets; implements; assesses; and coordinates security policies, processes, and procedures in matters related to personnel security, physical security, cyber security, information security, and industrial security programs.
	301	Miscellaneous Administration and Program (Subset)	Information management analyst: responsible for day-to-day operations involving cyber security tasks and identifying, resolving, and eliminating events that may lead to possible system threats. Personnel holding this position also recommend modifications to agency security plans and evaluate system goals, objectives, and priorities.
	343	Management and Program Analysis (Subset)	Management and program analyst (Infrastructure Security Compliance Division; the series includes two discrete positions)
			Mission Support: This position entails developing and tracking budgets; answering questions regarding vision and requirements of new spending; negotiating cost and logistics of new training; coordinating sponsored training; aligning new hires to billets; tracking personnel actions; supporting the reception of new staff; and developing operating procedures for training, hiring, or acquisitions.
			Policy: This position entails conducting outreach programs, responding to external inquiries, summarizing programs operations data, revising tools and policies, drafting regulations, reviewing inspection documents, managing programs, and issuing orders mandating compliance to delinquent facilities.
			Program analyst (Cybersecurity & Communications [CS&C]): provides acquisition strategy and plays a major role involving information technology (IT) procurement; plans, develops and manages administrative functions related to the efficiency and effectiveness of the enterprise acquisition system; and studies and interprets legislation, policy statements, rules, regulations, directives and other regulatory material to determine their intent and effect on operations.

Component			MCO
	Series	**Occupation**	**Job description**
	391	Telecommunication (Subset)	Telecommunications specialist (CS&C): ensures the accuracy of the telecommunications service priority database; resolves system support and telecommunications interface problems; briefs senior federal executives, emergency responder organizations, and communications sector private industry entities on Telecommunications Service Priority Program functions and initiatives.
	854	Computer Engineer	Computer engineer (NPPD-wide): provides advice and guidance on the implementation of systems engineering processes, and formulates, develops, and administers NPPD systems engineering process, planning and technology. Computer engineer (CS&C): manages, supervises, leads, or performs professional engineering and scientific work involving the design, construction, and operation of computer systems, including hardware and software and their integration.
	855	Electronics Engineer	Electronics engineer (CS&C): manages, supervises, leads, and performs professional engineering and scientific work for purposes such as communication, computation, sensing, control, measurement, and navigation.
	1550	Computer Science (Subset)	Computer scientist: responsible for the application of, or research into, computer science methods and techniques to store, manipulate, transform, or present information by means of computer systems. The position develops software, high-speed computing, real-time data acquisition, computer graphics, and integrated computer systems.

Component			MCO
	Series	Occupation	Job description
	1801	General Inspection, Investigation, & Compliance	Border and transportation security officer (NPPD-wide): reviews existing and proposed legislative and regulatory requirements and translates requirements of new legislation; recommends program development, planning, coordination, direction, and assessment activities relating to immigration eligibility; formulates interdiction policies, procedures, and guidelines; validates program studies and assessments; provides technical and operational guidance for operations; and evaluates efficiency and effectiveness for special projects programs.
			Chemical security inspector (Office of Infrastructure Protection): functions as subject matter expert on physical and technical security protective measures and procedures, and in reviewing and evaluating chemical facility physical, personnel, information and cyber security plans and countermeasures; plans, coordinates, participates in, or leads joint team inspections and compliance audits, including preparing field, compliance assistance and after-action reports; responsible for chemical facility situational awareness and management, emergency preparedness, and critical incident management.
			Protective security advisor (Office of Infrastructure Protection): serves as liaison among Department of Homeland Security (DHS) and other federal agencies, state and local government, and the private sector on critical infrastructure security compliance matters; functions as an expert on physical security protective measures and procedures; reviews and interprets directives, program changes, legal initiatives and DHS guidelines; and develops and implements local critical infrastructure policies, procedures and directives.
	1811	Criminal Investigation(Subset)	Criminal Investigator (Federal Protective Service [FPS]): conducts criminal and administrative investigations, plans and coordinates investigative processes, serves as case agent for interagency investigations, and may lead teams of criminal investigators and law enforcement officers. Personnel holding this position also provide coordination and guidance for mult jurisdictional and interregional investigations and prepare reports of investigation and intelligence studies and direct and coordinate working groups on law enforcement activities and intelligence issues.

Component	MCO		
	Series	**Occupation**	**Job description**
	2210	Information Technology (Subset)	Information technology specialist (CS&C): functions as a technical expert in two or more assigned areas, including policy and planning, security, application software, operating systems, network service, data management, systems administration, and customer support. Personnel in this position are responsible for planning, designing, adapting, developing, acquiring, documenting, testing, implementing, integrating, maintaining and modifying systems.
			Information technology specialist (U.S.–Computer Emergency Readiness Team): oversees and coordinates response to cyber incidents, provides on-site incident response, advises on strategies to protect and secure sensitive information and systems, monitors and plans for change in federal IT security policy and legislation, and analyzes and responds to software and hardware vulnerabilities. Personnel in this position are also responsible for interfacing with the DHS National Operations Center during cyber incidents and implementing IT security projects and initiatives.
			Information technology specialist (Network Security Deployment): develops deployment strategies for and leads efforts to coordinate and install cyber security network equipment and software at federal facilities, conducts testing, monitors network architecture and transmission protocols, and resolves cyber security network issues. Personnel in this position also identify network requirements, define and maintain network architecture, and determine the configuration and optimization of network cyber security installations.
Transportation Security Administration (TSA)	132	Intelligence	Intelligence officer: provides intelligence support and threat briefings; liaises with the Joint Terrorism Task Forces and state, local, and tribal law enforcement officials and intelligence fusion centers; serves as a technical advisor; contributes to the development of high-level briefs and detailed and complex studies.
	340	Program Management (Federal Security Director Subset)	Federal security director: provides day-to-day direction for federal airport security staff and operations for an airport. The federal security director is responsible for supporting security evolution and ensuring the deployment, management, and oversight of people, processes, and technology to improve security operations. The federal security director is the primary ranking TSA authority responsible for leadership and coordination of TSA security activities.

Component	MCO		
	Series	Occupation	Job description
	1801	General Inspection, Investigation, & Compliance	Transportation security inspector: conducts regulatory inspections/investigations and supports criminal investigations related to alleged or suspected security violations by identifying, collecting, and preserving evidence used to support enforcement actions.
			Federal air marshal: primary duty is to investigate, apprehend, or detain individuals suspected or convicted of offenses against the criminal law of U.S. air carriers, airports, crews, and passengers.
	1802	Compliance Inspection and Support	Transportation security officer: performs all security functions related to the screening of people, property, and cargo through the use and application of procedures, techniques, and technology.
	1811	Criminal Investigation	Criminal investigator: conducts, monitors, and coordinates criminal and administrative investigations and inspections; responds to security violations; interviews and interrogates witnesses and suspects; reviews transportation security measures and operations; identifies problem areas and recommends solutions; documents violations and prepares criminal and civil cases; and tests security systems for compliance.
United States Citizenship and Immigration Services (USCIS)	1801	General Inspection, Investigation, & Compliance (Immigration Services Officer Subset)	Immigration services officer: responsible for the adjudication of applications and petitions for benefits and privileges. Personnel in the position also perform assignments in the following areas: data integrity, security, customer support, liaison, communications, interviews, analysis, and training.
United States Secret Service (USSS)	80	Security Administration (Physical Security Specialist (Law Enforcement) Subset)	Physical security specialist: plans, develops, and implements a comprehensive technical security program for major protective advance trips involving designated protectees, and conducts technical investigative support functions and activities in the United States and overseas. The position holder also serves as agency technical authority in one of the technical security specialized programs and senior technical advisor for large-scale protective activities.
	83	Police	Officer (Uniformed Division): ensures the protection of officials and their families, designated embassies, and other specified federal property; enforces laws, statutes, and ordinances; investigates accidents and crimes; arrests suspects; and appears in court. The position also covers designated security posts, preparation of incident reports, response to security alarms, and interviews of unauthorized persons seeking admission to protected areas.
			Sergeant, lieutenant, captain, deputy/assistant chief, and chief perform, supervise or manage duties above and, depending upon position, engage in planning, policy development, and administration of Uniformed Division activities and operations.

Component			MCO
	Series	Occupation	Job description
	1802	Compliance Inspection and Support (Special Officer/Physical Security Subset)	Protective support technician: performs driving and technical protective support duties associated with the security of protective operations and movements and the secure transportation of armored vehicles used in those movements.
			Special officer: maintains designated protective security posts; inspects all operational, safety, emergency, and convenience equipment of protective vehicles to ensure peak operating condition; drives protective vehicle or follow-up; controls the movement of persons into and around multiple Secret Service facilities and associated areas; monitors and operates various communications equipment; and employs various advanced X-ray screening technologies in order to detect and identify high-risk items.
	1811	Criminal Investigation	Criminal investigator: investigates specified violations of U.S. laws, performs security surveys and background investigations, and works with U.S. Attorneys in preparing and presenting federal cases. Protection duties include advance security surveys of domestic locations, covering designated security posts, and keeping close to designated protectees.

Source: GAO analysis of DHS data.

Appendix II: Comments from the Department of Homeland Security

U.S. Department of Homeland Security
Washington, DC 20528

Homeland Security

September 9, 2013

David C. Maurer
Director, Homeland Security and Justice
U.S. Government Accountability Office
441 G Street, NW
Washington, DC 20548

Re: Draft Report GAO-13-742, "DHS RECRUITING AND HIRING: DHS is Generally
       Filling Mission Critical Positions, but Could Better Track Costs of Coordinated
       Recruiting Efforts"

Dear Mr. Maurer,

Thank you for the opportunity to review and comment on this draft report. The U.S. Department
of Homeland Security (DHS) appreciates the U.S. Government Accountability Office's (GAO's)
work in planning and conducting its review and issuing this report.

We are pleased to note GAO's recognition of the Department's efforts to develop and implement
the DHS Coordinated Recruiting and Outreach Strategy (CROS) for Fiscal Years 2012–2017).
The CROS provides DHS with an efficient approach to filling its mission critical occupations
with high caliber talent.

The draft report contained one recommendation for executive action, and DHS concurs.
Specifically, GAO recommended that the Secretary of Homeland Security direct the Office of
the Chief Human Capital Officer (OCHCO) to:

Recommendation 1: Require all components to provide OCHCO Diversity and Inclusion
(D&I) with recruiting cost information in a consistent manner to allow better tracking of overall
recruiting costs and use this information to assess the extent to which recruiting costs are being
reduced by components as a result of increased coordination and leveraging resources as called
for in the CROS.

Response: Concur. OCHCO D&I will work through the DHS Corporate Recruitment Council
(CRC) to develop and implement a system to consistently track and analyze overall recruiting
costs. The CRC is led by the D&I National Recruitment Advisor and is composed of
Component representation throughout the Department, including Headquarters. Moving
forward, all Components will be required to provide D&I with recruiting cost information in a
consistent manner to allow better tracking of overall recruiting costs. This information will
enable the Department to assess the extent to which recruiting costs are being reduced by
Components as a result of increased coordination, as called for in the CROS. Estimated
Completion Date: December 31, 2013.

Again, thank you for the opportunity to review and comment on this draft report. Technical comments were provided under separate cover. Please feel free to contact me if you have any questions. We look forward to working with you in the future.

Sincerely,

Jim H. Crumpacker
Director
Departmental GAO-OIG Liaison Office

2

Appendix III: GAO Contact and Staff Acknowledgments

GAO Contact	David C. Maurer, (202) 512-9627 or maurerd@gao.gov
Staff Acknowledgments	In addition to the contact named above, Adam Hoffman, Assistant Director; Adam Couvillion, Analyst-in-Charge; Dave Bieler; Chris Ferencik; Christine Hanson; Tracey King; Lara Miklozek; and Amanda Miller made significant contributions to the work.